This coloring book is dedicated to my greatest inspirations. To my mentor Angel Claudio, thank you for showing me the magic that is fashion. May you continue to watch over me. To my aunt Rosa (Miss Diva) for being my first muse and introducing me into the world of fashion. To my muse and runway daughter Jalen. You are always a source of inspiration for all of my designs, my personal Barbie doll. Lastly and most important my mother for teaching me that anything is possible because of you I am. You may have prayed for me but I chose you long before. My mother like no other.

"I DON'T DESIGN
CLOTHES. I DESIGN
DREAMS."
-RALPH LAUREN-

"FASHIONS FADE, STYLE
IS ETERNAL."
—YVES SAINT LAURENT—

"I THINK THERE IS BEAUTY
IN EVERYTHING. WHAT
'NORMAL' PEOPLE
PERCEIVE AS UGLY, I CAN
USUALLY SEE SOMETHING
OF BEAUTY IN IT."
—ALEXANDER MCQUEEN—

"IN DIFFICULT TIMES,
FASHION IS ALWAYS
OUTRAGEOUS."
—ELSA SCHIAPARELLI—

DON'T BE INTO TRENDS.
DON'T MAKE FASHION
OWN YOU, BUT YOU
DECIDE WHAT YOU ARE,
WHAT YOU WANT TO
EXPRESS BY THE WAY
YOU DRESS AND THE
WAY TO LIVE."
— <u>GIANNI VERSACE</u> —

"FASHION IS VERY IMPORTANT. IT IS LIFE-ENHANCING AND, LIKE EVERYTHING THAT GIVES PLEASURE, IT IS WORTH DOING WELL."

—VIVIENNE WESTWOOD—

"FASHION IS THE ARMOR
TO SURVIVE THE REALITY
OF EVERYDAY LIFE."
—BILL CUNNINGHAM—

"THE DRESS MUST
FOLLOW THE BODY OF
A WOMAN, NOT THE
BODY FOLLOWING THE
SHAPE OF THE DRESS."
—HUBERT DE GIVENCHY—

"IN ORDER TO BE
IRREPLACEABLE ONE
MUST ALWAYS BE
DIFFERENT."
—<u>COCO CHANEL</u>—

ELEGANCE IS NOT
STANDING OUT, BUT
BEING REMEMBERED."
—GIORGIO ARMANI—

"WE MUST NEVER CONFUSE
ELEGANCE WITH SNOBBERY."
—YVES SAINT LAURENT —

"I WANT PEOPLE TO SEE THE DRESS, BUT FOCUS ON THE WOMAN."
—VERA WANG —

I MAKE CLOTHES,
WOMEN MAKE FASHION."
— AZZEDINE ALAÏA —

"OVER THE YEARS I HAVE LEARNED THAT WHAT IS IMPORTANT IN A DRESS IS THE WOMAN WHO'S WEARING IT."
—<u>YVES SAINT LAURENT</u>—

"THE GRATIFICATION OF TURNING SOMETHING DULL INTO SOMETHING BRIGHT IS WHAT EXCITES ME. THE ABILITY TO PLAY WITH COLOR, SHAPES AND JUST ABOUT ANYTHING TO BUILD WHAT I SEE AS BEAUTIFUL IS WHAT I OPEN MY EYES TO DO. TO BE ABLE TO USE MY HANDS TO TELL A STORY IS WHAT I WAS BORN TO DO. I AM A DESIGNER"

-AMORE "WILLIAM" AYALA-

About the Designer

Amore William Ayala (Thee Amour) Newark NJ's own. A self-taught fashion designer, designing since the fourth grade. Discovered by his aunt Rosa Garcia (Miss Diva), an aspiring singer and model. Amore started his career as a child model learning all he could on and off the runways. From model training, creative director work and styling for numerous productions. Under the guidance and direction of his aunt and Tyrone Chablis (NJ Fashion Designer) and later his Mentor and greatest inspiration, Angel Claudio (NJ Fashion Designer), who sadly passed away in 2005.

His fashion brand Sew Style Hause & AYALA Couture meets high glamour and fantasy perfectly in the middle. A mixture of high-end couture pieces and comfortable yet stylish urban wear. Sew Style Hause a sewing pattern company that specializes in easy to make patterns with high end looks for the self-taught and beginner designer/seamstress. Helping designers everywhere achieve their design dreams and potential. Being self-taught himself he understood how discouraging sewing could be without training and the lack of pattern styles for his types of designs. His by appointment only showroom is a must see fantasy.

All designs, creative concepts and styling by
Amore "William" Ayala

Illustrations by Iana

Hair inspired by: @Marcoswigs

9 798218 048938